M000249596

Ethereum Projects for Beginners

Build blockchain-based cryptocurrencies, smart contracts, and DApps

Kenny Vaneetvelde

BIRMINGHAM - MUMBAI

Ethereum Projects for Beginners

Commissioning Editor: Pavan Ramchandani
Acquisition Editor: Namrata Patil
Content Development Editors: Rhea Henriques, Unnati Guha
Technical Editor: Dharmendra Yadav
Copy Editor: Safis Editing
Project Coordinator: Kirti Pisat
Proofreader: Safis Editing
Indexer: Tejal Daruwale Soni
Graphics: Jisha Chirayil
Production Coordinator: Aparna Bhagat

First published: July 2018

Production reference: 1230718

Published by Packt Publishing Ltd.
Livery Place
35 Livery Street
Birmingham
B3 2PB, UK.

ISBN 978-1-78953-740-6

www.packtpub.com

`mapt.io`

Mapt is an online digital library that gives you full access to over 5,000 books and videos, as well as industry leading tools to help you plan your personal development and advance your career. For more information, please visit our website.

Why subscribe?

- Spend less time learning and more time coding with practical eBooks and Videos from over 4,000 industry professionals

- Improve your learning with Skill Plans built especially for you

- Get a free eBook or video every month

- Mapt is fully searchable

- Copy and paste, print, and bookmark content

PacktPub.com

Did you know that Packt offers eBook versions of every book published, with PDF and ePub files available? You can upgrade to the eBook version at `www.PacktPub.com` and as a print book customer, you are entitled to a discount on the eBook copy. Get in touch with us at `service@packtpub.com` for more details.

At `www.PacktPub.com`, you can also read a collection of free technical articles, sign up for a range of free newsletters, and receive exclusive discounts and offers on Packt books and eBooks.

Contributor

About the author

Kenny Vaneetvelde had been trading Bitcoin for a few years when he heard about a new technology called Ethereum and was completely captivated by it. After learning all that he could about Ethereum and other blockchain technologies that had suddenly started sprouting up everywhere, he spent over a year doing R and D, developing prototypes, and training new employees in a consultancy firm so that they could start up a new blockchain branch.

Packt is searching for authors like you

If you're interested in becoming an author for Packt, please visit `authors.packtpub.com` and apply today. We have worked with thousands of developers and tech professionals, just like you, to help them share their insight with the global tech community. You can make a general application, apply for a specific hot topic that we are recruiting an author for, or submit your own idea.

Table of Contents

Preface

This book is designed to give you an insight into the world of Ethereum blockchain and enables you to make your own cryptocurrency using Ethereum. Throughout this book, you will be learning about various concepts and applying that knowledge directly, while also being introduced to the wide scope of functionality that Ethereum blockchain will be providing in the future.

Who this book is for

If you are anyone who is passionate about knowing how blockchain works, or if you are an enthusiast who wishes to work on cryptocurrencies or has an interest in hacking, then this book is meant for you.

What this book covers

Chapter 1, *Workflow Setup and Thinking Blockchain*, focuses on recapping the basics of Ethereum blockchain. We will go through some examples and real-life projects, trying to get you into that blockchain mindset. Then, we will set up the workflow, and the tooling around it, using npm.

Chapter 2, *Developing Your First Decentralized Application with Ethereum*, looks at developing your first payment application with Ethereum.

Chapter 3, *Creating Your Own Cryptocurrency on the Ethereum Blockchain*, takes you through how to create your own cryptocurrency on top of Ethereum blockchain.

Chapter 4, *Signing Legal Documents on Blockchains and Identity Verification*, will show you how you can work with legal documents and identity on Ethereum blockchain.

Chapter 5, *Ethereum Outside the PC/Web Environment*, explores how you can use Ethereum outside PC or web environments. We will also look at some further steps and where you can take all these lessons from here.

To get the most out of this book

Knowledge of at least one object-oriented language is required. It's very good if you know some JavaScript.

We are going to make extensive use of NPM, and we are going to recap the basics of blockchain, but some prior basic knowledge is always beneficial, of course.

Download the example code files

You can download the example code files for this book from your account at www.packtpub.com. If you purchased this book elsewhere, you can visit www.packtpub.com/support and register to have the files emailed directly to you.

You can download the code files by following these steps:

1. Log in or register at www.packtpub.com.
2. Select the **SUPPORT** tab.
3. Click on **Code Downloads & Errata**.
4. Enter the name of the book in the **Search** box and follow the onscreen instructions.

Once the file is downloaded, please make sure that you unzip or extract the folder using the latest version of:

- WinRAR/7-Zip for Windows
- Zipeg/iZip/UnRarX for Mac
- 7-Zip/PeaZip for Linux

The code bundle for the book is also hosted on GitHub at https://github.com/PacktPublishing/Ethereum-Projects-for-Beginners. In case there's an update to the code, it will be updated on the existing GitHub repository.

We also have other code bundles from our rich catalog of books and videos available at https://github.com/PacktPublishing/. Check them out!

Conventions used

There are a number of text conventions used throughout this book.

`CodeInText`: Indicates code words in text, database table names, folder names, filenames, file extensions, pathnames, dummy URLs, user input, and Twitter handles. Here is an example: "This can be done by typing `ganache-cli` in the terminal window."

A block of code is set as follows:

```
function MetaCoin() public {
    balances[tx.origin] = 10000;
}
```

Any command-line input or output is written as follows:

```
C:\Windows\System32\my_project>truffle-cli compile
```

Bold: Indicates a new term, an important word, or words that you see on screen. For example, words in menus or dialog boxes appear in the text like this. Here is an example: "Type in the localhost URL mentioned previously and click **Save**."

 Warnings or important notes appear like this.

 Tips and tricks appear like this.

Get in touch

Feedback from our readers is always welcome.

General feedback: Email `feedback@packtpub.com` and mention the book title in the subject of your message. If you have questions about any aspect of this book, please email us at `questions@packtpub.com`.

Errata: Although we have taken every care to ensure the accuracy of our content, mistakes do happen. If you have found a mistake in this book, we would be grateful if you would report this to us. Please visit www.packtpub.com/submit-errata, selecting your book, clicking on the Errata Submission Form link, and entering the details.

Piracy: If you come across any illegal copies of our works in any form on the Internet, we would be grateful if you would provide us with the location address or website name. Please contact us at copyright@packtpub.com with a link to the material.

If you are interested in becoming an author: If there is a topic that you have expertise in and you are interested in either writing or contributing to a book, please visit authors.packtpub.com.

Reviews

Please leave a review. Once you have read and used this book, why not leave a review on the site that you purchased it from? Potential readers can then see and use your unbiased opinion to make purchase decisions, we at Packt can understand what you think about our products, and our authors can see your feedback on their book. Thank you!

For more information about Packt, please visit packtpub.com.

Workflow Setup and Thinking Blockchain 1

Blockchains are the new fad in the word of cryptocurrency; we have witnessed the remarkably growing popularity of Bitcoins. Ethereum uses a technology similar to Bitcoin, and the coin that it trades in is known as **ether**. There is not much difference between the two except for smart contracts that are nothing but the codes that are written using the **Ethereum Virtual Machine (EVM)**, which automates as well as executes agreements in an immutable ledger. We will get to know more about this later. To dive in further, first we are going to go over some use cases—they're very interesting. Next we will provide an overview of the Ethereum blockchain and blockchain in general. We will look at some of the benefits and limitations of blockchain. Then, we are going to get into setting up an efficient workflow so that we can get into further chapters without anything holding us back.

Topics that we'll be covering in this chapter are as follows:

- Ethereum-based projects
- An overview of blockchain and Ethereum
- Benefits and limitations
- Setting up an efficient workflow

Ethereum-based projects

Ethereum is like Bitcoin, but it's for code! It's the blockchain for smart contracts and it stores immutable code and logic in the blockchain. Immutable is a very important word here. That's pretty much all you need to know about Ethereum. So, what's possible right now? Let's have a look in the following sections.

Gnosis

Gnosis is market-driven forecasting technology. It is based on proven scientific research. It has its own platform known as the Gnosis platform and you can build your own platform on top of it. It basically makes trading predictions. And correct predictions are given the tokens that were at stake for incorrect predictions. Visit `https://gnosis.pm/` to access Gnosis.

The way it works is that you trade predictions or you bet on predictions. The following is the front page of Gnosis:

Gnosis front page

In the preceding screenshot, do note the question that is being asked on their home page. Will Dubai's world record for the largest New Year's Eve fireworks display get broken? You can vote yes or no, and by voting, your tokens are at stake, and an Oracle is then going to tell you whether the event happened or not. The blockchain will then check on that Oracle. Oracles are nothing but smart contracts that interact with the outside elements. They can store and retrieve data—this is just what an Ethereum transaction needs to make decisions. An Oracle is a trusted source, and after checking with this trusted source, you can determine in a blockchain whether the event really did happen or not, and you can be absolutely certain about it.

The following diagram explains exactly how this happens:

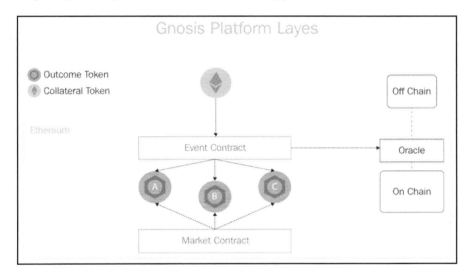

The Gnosis platform layers

FirstBlood

FirstBlood is comparable to Gnosis; it is for e-sports. In cases where you are a gamer, you can sign up for a match using tokens. You can put tokens at stake to win tokens, you can put yourself in a queue in a pool of other teams or people, and you can play against them. You can even participate in tournaments. The winner of the game gets the tokens. Oracle is used to decide the outcome of a match. Visit `http://firstblood.io` to access FirstBlood.

Dynamis

This is a peer-to-peer insurance company, meaning there are no more middlemen. Currently, they are working on unemployment insurance, wherein you get paid to be unemployed! You just have to show people that you are actively looking for a job. The way they verify this is by using an Oracle similar to Gnosis and FirstBlood, but they use it to check LinkedIn and to verify that you have been applying to jobs.

To learn more about Dynamis visit, `www.dynamisapp.com`.

You can also visit `http://blog.dynamisapp.com/p2p-insurance-solutions/` to gain further insight.

Ujo Music

This is basically a decentralized music store for artists! We all know iTunes, Spotify, and so on. These are companies that are sitting in the middle of artists and their fans, but fans can't know right away how much money artists actually make from each sale. Ujo Music takes care of this by decentralizing the music store. There are no more middlemen, which means that they are a bridge between artists and fan. This certainly means it ensures more power and money for the artists. There are no worries about licensing and it delivers music services only to verified identities. To access Ujo Music, visit `https://ujomusic.com/`.

The way it works work is described in the screenshot; they have multiple layers and they have their licensing and payments on Ethereum. They have a persistent identity on uPort which is also built on Ethereum:

Ujo Music

The files themselves are stored in decentralized file storage, **InterPlanetary File System (IPFS)**, and the metadata uses constellate which is also built on Ethereum.

The next project is one of my favorites.

Golem

It is a decentralized supercomputer! It does off-chain calculations. Off-chain calculations are calculations that do not happen on the blockchain; calculations are done outside of the blockchain. Then on the on-chain, it will verify these calculations. This means you can rent out your spare computing power or you can hire extra computing power if you need it. You can do this for 3D rendering, computational chemistry, AI machine learning—anything you like. To visit Golem, go to `https://golem.network/`.

In the following screenshot, you can see the Golem GUI. On the left, you can see a basic wallet; you can also see how much CPU, RAM, and disk space are being used. To the right, you can see a little proof of concept of three tasks being put out there, it's three Blender tasks, in this case, 3D rendering tasks:

Golem GUI

Overview of blockchain and Ethereum

Here, we will provide a short overview of Ethereum and blockchain in general. We will have a little look under the hood so that you can get a better understanding of how Ethereum and blockchain make these great products—these great use cases that we've seen are possible.

Going from Bitcoin to Ethereum

Bitcoin was the first blockchain, but Bitcoin was only meant for payments. People started discovering that Bitcoin could be used for other scenarios; we call this **Colored Coins**. Bitcoin had a surprisingly open design and one guy, Vitalik Buterin, decided to start developing Ethereum on top of the Bitcoin blockchain. But, due to limitations in Bitcoin, Ethereum now has its own blockchain.

The following table shows the differences between Bitcoin and Ethereum:

Bitcoin	Ethereum
Used for payments	Used for code and logic
It is a digital currency	It is a smart contract platform
Average block time/transaction processing time of 10 minutes	Average block time/transaction processing time of only 17.5 seconds
It is not Turing complete	It is Turing complete

Bitcoin and Ethereum are both blockchains. They both rely heavily on private/public-key cryptography, and even though Bitcoin is primarily a form of payment, both can be used to transfer value, although, with the Ethereum blockchain, value will be processed with logic. Both are completely immutable.

The following are the things to remember for blockchains:

- When something is in the blockchain, it's final. That means there's no rolling back of anything you do, so even with your code, you have to find special way to update it.
- Your private key is your digital identity, so don't lose it!
- Blockchain is not standalone; it's usually used in conjunction with other technologies, mostly frontend technology or backend technology.

The benefits and limitations

Now that we've looked at an overview of blockchain, we will be having a look at some of the benefits of blockchain. We will also have a look at some of the limitations when you are developing a blockchain application, and we will have a look at how we can overcome these limitations or how we can work around them.

Benefits of blockchain and Ethereum

The following are some of the benefits of blockchain:

- Decentralization
- Trustlessness—you don't have to trust or put all your money in a single point of failure
- It can be very cost effective
- It can also present itself to be the backbone of IoT and electric vehicles, a power grid, or a decentralized identity in your smartphone or an electric ID card

Limitations of blockchain and Ethereum

The following are some difficulties one can face while using blockchains:

- If you try to use blockchain where you don't need it, it can be very costly.
- Blockchains don't really do private data that well because blockchains are supposed to be public.
- Sometimes, centralization is required, and blockchains are always decentralized; that doesn't fit.
- Most blockchains don't really scale well to high usage.
- Storing big files is not really recommended because more computation means more power and more money on a public blockchain; on a private blockchain it just means more power—and you need to invest more in your infrastructure so that is also more money.

Overcoming limitations

Sometimes, you just can't overcome limitations because you just have to use blockchain where you need it. Some things can be overcome, such as storing private data on a public chain. This can be done by adding some extra encryption to your data. You can store big files on the IPFS which is also decentralized—it is not a blockchain, but it is decentralized file storage and it works really well with Ethereum. The problem of scalability is solved by Ethereum's sharding: sharding means splitting the space of accounts, such as contracts, into smaller subspaces. Private chains are also available if you need them, such as J.P. Morgan's Quorum, Monax, and Bletchley. They are all Ethereum based.

Setting up the workflow

Here, we will be doing some workflow setup so we can get started with developing.

Requirements

The following are the things we will need for setting up the workflow:

- Google Chrome.
- MetaMask, which is a Chrome extension. We will use this to connect to and to test the blockchain.
- **Node Package Manager (NPM)**.
- Truffle, which is our first framework. We will be using it to develop our first decentralized application.
- Ethereum-JS ganache-cli, which is a test blockchain.

Getting started

Follow these steps to set up the workflow:

1. Get the NPM. It is part of Node.js. You can get it at `www.npmjs.com/get-npm`, as shown in the following screenshot:

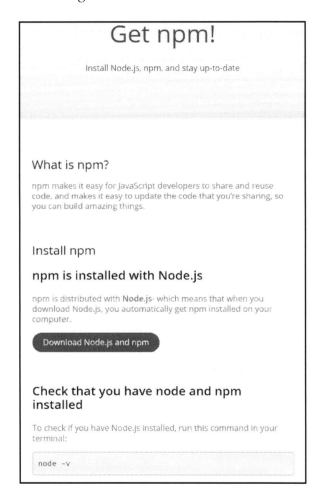

Getting the NPM

2. Select the latest version displayed on their web page:
   - Install MetaMask. To download MetaMask, visit `https://metamask.io/`.

3. Click on **GET CHROME EXTENSION**.
   - Then click on **Add to Chrome**.

4. The preceding tool that we will be used to test our blockchain applications. Once you've installed it, a new tab will open up with a video explaining in depth how to use it and what it is.

5. It is important for you to remember during this book that you can connect to the main network as well as three test networks, but you can also set up your own network, your own blockchain, and run on that. The following screenshot shows this:

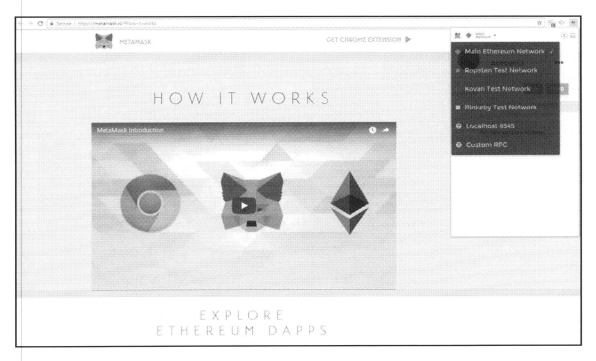

MetaMask Main Network

6. Install the Ethereum blockchain simulator called `ganache-cli`.
7. This can be done as explained in the following screenshot:

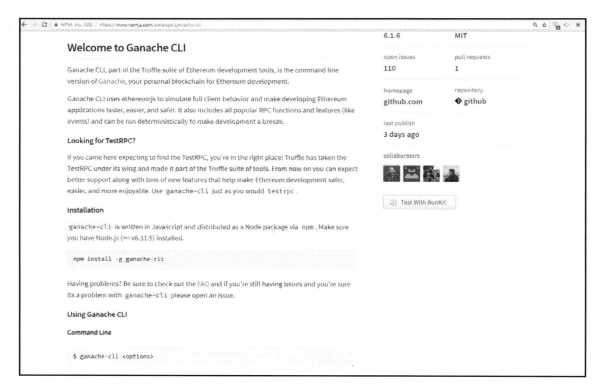

Command to install Ethereum blockchain simulator

8. You can install this as a node package by just copying this command and pasting it in your terminal. Once you've pasted it in your terminal, it will start installing, as shown here:

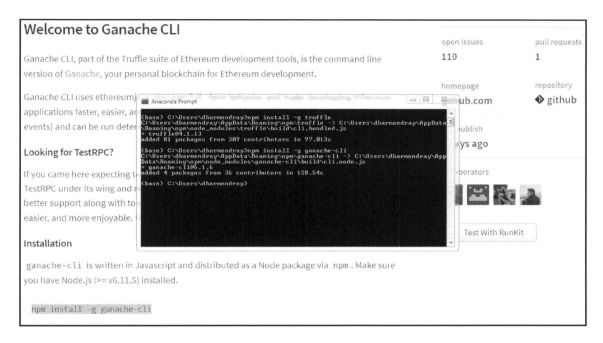

Installing Ethereum Simulator

Once that is done, it will tell you that it has succeeded; quit this for now because I have already reinstalled this. You can go ahead and verify it by typing `ganache-cli` into your Command Prompt and verifying that it runs. The following will be the output you will get if you have installed the simulator correctly:

Ethereum Simulator

9. Installing and downloading Truffle.
10. Truffle also is a simple node package from `truffleframework.com` that you can install by copying and pasting a command into your terminal, as shown here:

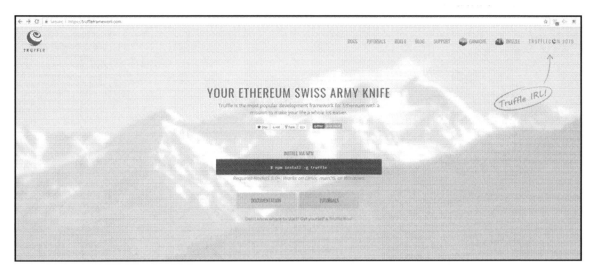

Command for installing Truffle

11. Once that's done installing, you can verify it by typing `truffle`, as shown in the following screenshot, and now you can use any of these commands:

```
Anaconda Prompt
==================
6721975

Listening on 127.0.0.1:8545
>
(base) C:\Users\dharmendray>truffle
Truffle v4.1.13 - a development framework for Ethereum

Usage: truffle <command> [options]

Commands:
  init       Initialize new and empty Ethereum project
  compile    Compile contract source files
  migrate    Run migrations to deploy contracts
  deploy     (alias for migrate)
  build      Execute build pipeline (if configuration present)
  test       Run JavaScript and Solidity tests
  debug      Interactively debug any transaction on the blockchain (experimental)

  opcode     Print the compiled opcodes for a given contract
  console    Run a console with contract abstractions and commands available
  develop    Open a console with a local development blockchain
  create     Helper to create new contracts, migrations and tests
  install    Install a package from the Ethereum Package Registry
  publish    Publish a package to the Ethereum Package Registry
  networks   Show addresses for deployed contracts on each network
  watch      Watch filesystem for changes and rebuild the project automatically
  serve      Serve the build directory on localhost and watch for changes
  exec       Execute a JS module within this Truffle environment
  unbox      Download a Truffle Box, a pre-built Truffle project
  version    Show version number and exit

See more at http://truffleframework.com/docs

(base) C:\Users\dharmendray>
```

Truffle

12. You can use `init` to initialize a new project, which we will be doing in the next chapter. Hence, we have successfully completed the installation.

Summary

We have discussed different projects running on Ethereum and gained an overview of blockchain; after this, we moved on to its benefits and limitations, and how to overcome the limitations. In the end, we created a setup for our own Ethereum workflow.

In the next chapter, we will be developing our first simple decentralized payment application with Ethereum.

2
Developing Your First Decentralized Application with Ethereum

DApps or a **Decentralized applications** is an application that is run on a blockchain. Ethereum provides its users with some flexibility that allows them to create such applications. In this chapter, we will focus on creating a DApp and learn how to implement it in various aspects of our lives.

In this chapter, we will learn how to do the following:

- Create a project
- Deploying and testing a project
- Explore the Solidity syntax and JavaScript codes
- Bug fixing and debugging smart contracts
- Changing our application with a better payment method

In order to build an application, we need to understand the codes and syntax that are used to develop it. Hence, we will take a look at the Solidity syntax and also understand the working of the JavaScript codes.

Creating a project

This section will teach us how to create a new project. It will require us to explore the code and the Solidity syntax. Deploying the project will help us understand how easy it is to transform this project into a better payment application. To get a better understanding of the concept, we are going to take a look at some specifics on bug fixing and also learn to debug smart contracts and some function applications.

To begin, we need to create a new folder. For convention's sake, let's name this `my_first_project`.

The immediate next step would be to run Truffle. The following command is used for this:

```
C:\WINDOWS\system32>truffle
```

The output of the command should be as follows:

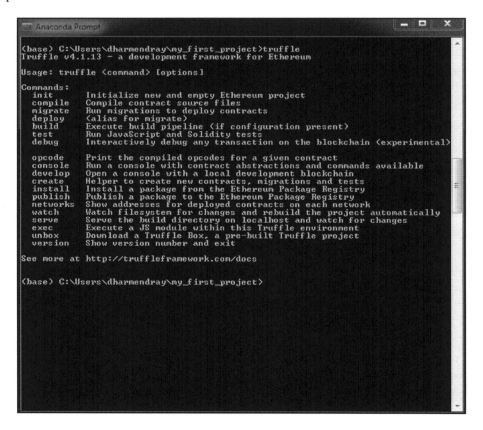

This displays the list of commands that can be used for various processes for Truffle. The Truffle `init` command allows us to initialize a new Truffle project.

Throughout the book, we will use a handy Truffle unbox command which will download and set up a boilerplate project. For this, we will use the `webpack` box, which is done by running the `truffle unbox webpack` command as shown in the following screenshot:

```
C:\Windows\System32\my_project>truffle unbox webpack
```

All the boxes are listed on their website and it is a growing list, among which there are some React boxes and many others. The unboxing takes a while, after which you will see the following message on your screen:

```
Select Administrator: Command Prompt                                    —  □  ×
develop    Open a console with a local development blockchain
create     Helper to create new contracts, migrations and tests
install    Install a package from the Ethereum Package Registry
publish    Publish a package to the Ethereum Package Registry
networks   Show addresses for deployed contracts on each network
watch      Watch filesystem for changes and rebuild the project automatically
serve      Serve the build directory on localhost and watch for changes
exec       Execute a JS module within this Truffle environment
unbox      Download a Truffle Box, a pre-built Truffle project
version    Show version number and exit

See more at http://truffleframework.com/docs


C:\Windows\System32\my_project>truffle unbox webpack
Downloading...
Unpacking...
Setting up...
Unbox successful. Sweet!

Commands:

  Compile:              truffle compile
  Migrate:              truffle migrate
  Test contracts:       truffle test
  Run linter:           npm run lint
  Run dev server:       npm run dev
  Build for production:  npm run build

C:\Windows\System32\my_project>_
```

Once this is done, we can start creating our project in an editor of our choice. We can begin by examining the project structure. The unboxing will have created several files and folders for us. Your screen should look similar to the following:

It will also install a webpack, which can be configured through the `webpack.config.js` file. This file allows you to configure how you will minimize your JSON, CSS, and JavaScript, and everything in-between. You will also have a `truffle.js` file, which is used to define your networks. Upon clicking this, your screen will look as follows:

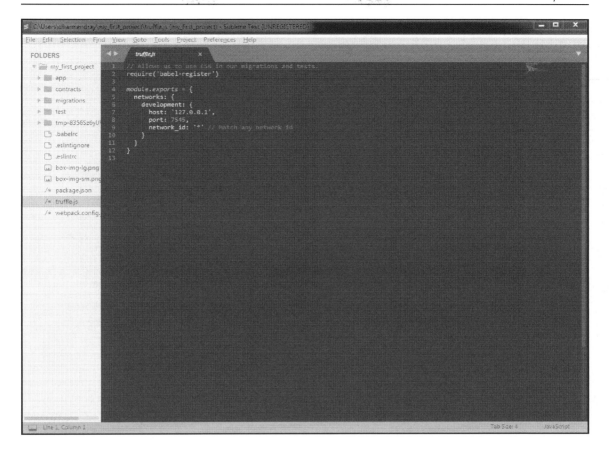

The `truffle.js` file comes predefined with a development network that defaults to a localhost on port `7545`. It will also create an app folder that contains our main project. This folder contains an index of HTML and some CSS and JavaScript that imports our smart contracts. The `contracts` folder contains `ConvertLib` which is a simple library for demonstration purposes that is imported inside of the `main` file, `MetaCoin.sol`. The file extension clearly depicts that the language used here is Solidity, which one might call a dialect of JavaScript that was developed for Ethereum. You can also see a migrations and `test` folder. Each serves its own purpose, which we shall learn during the course of the book. The next section will show us how to deploy and test a project.

Deploying and testing a projects

We will now be deploying the application that we created in the previous section. We will do so by starting a development blockchain, configuring our deployment, deploying our smart contracts, and building the application.

Starting a development blockchain

Firstly, we are going to want to run our development blockchain. This can be done by typing `ganache-cli` in the terminal window. Your screen will look as follows:

Make sure you jot down or remember the localhost port number. It is of importance, as you will be connecting to it in the later stages of this project. **Ganache-cli** generates 10 available accounts and then the corresponding private keys. These private keys are used to encrypt the transactions that are being sent from each individual account. At the bottom, you will see a **Mnemonic**. These twelve words are very important. Always remember to save these words because you will require them to import your private keys and the same accounts into MetaMask.

Configuring your deployment

Moving ahead, we need to make sure that the project settings are corresponding to the hostname and the port on which our blockchain was created. To do this, you need to go back to your editor, find the truffle.js file that is situated in the root folder, and change the port number here from 7545 to 8545 to match the port number that is hosting our development blockchain. There will be no need to make any changes to the host as that is just the localhost. Then, proceed to deploying your project on the terminal window, in the my_first_project folder. Use the following command:

```
C:\Windows\System32\my_project>truffle-cli compile
```

If you are using the Windows system we need to make some changes in the npm Package folder which will be located at C:/users/[YOUR USERNAME]/appdata/roaming/npm. The path may be vary depending upon where each user has installed the npm package different machine. We need to rename the truffle.cmd file to truffle-cli.cmd in the npm package.

This ensures that the smart contracts get compiled without any errors. Once this happens, your screen should look something as follows:

```
Administrator: Command Prompt                                                      —    □    ×

'truffle' is not recognized as an internal or external command,
operable program or batch file.

C:\Windows\System32\my_project>E:

E:\>cd chp2

E:\chp2>truffle-cli compile
Compiling .\contracts\ConvertLib.sol...
Compiling .\contracts\MetaCoin.sol...
Compiling .\contracts\Migrations.sol...

Compilation warnings encountered:

/E/chp2/contracts/MetaCoin.sol:15:2: Warning: Defining constructors as functions with the same name as the contract is d
eprecated. Use "constructor(...) { ... }" instead.
        function MetaCoin() public {
 ^ (Relevant source part starts here and spans across multiple lines).
,/E/chp2/contracts/Migrations.sol:11:3: Warning: Defining constructors as functions with the same name as the contract i
s deprecated. Use "constructor(...) { ... }" instead.
    function Migrations() public {
 ^ (Relevant source part starts here and spans across multiple lines}.
,/E/chp2/contracts/MetaCoin.sol:23:3: Warning: Invoking events without "emit" prefix is deprecated.
            Transfer(msg.sender, receiver, amount);
            ^-------------------------------------^

Writing artifacts to .\build\contracts

E:\chp2>_
```

The build output files have now been written in the contracts folder (also known as the `build` folder).

Deploying the smart contracts

The immediate next step would be to migrate and deploy these smart contracts to your development blockchain. To do this, we use the following command:

```
C:\Windows\System32\my_project>truffle-cli migrate
```

```
Administrator: Command Prompt                                                        —    □    ×

,/E/chp2/contracts/MetaCoin.sol:23:3: Warning: Invoking events without "emit" prefix is deprecated.
            Transfer(msg.sender, receiver, amount);
            ^-------------------------------------^

Writing artifacts to .\build\contracts


E:\chp2>truffle-cli migrate
Using network 'development'.

Running migration: 1_initial_migration.js
  Deploying Migrations...
  ... 0x14ea0ce35fbbd4d4a51be07893acd65eba58216dbc9622a54e703d8917b9d5c9
  Migrations: 0x0d108687467a1b232ade8ceac971a73c3dce5dd7
Saving successful migration to network...
  ... 0x9d18d99d4c7db5f10746ced59499c823d8d890059b05a4206e8f170ceb624b4a
Saving artifacts...
Running migration: 2_deploy_contracts.js
  Deploying ConvertLib...
  ... 0x48758cb68a941f24ed3ae2e1d8e5a1759e7f48a2b26726abe7f05f982f92ef7e
  ConvertLib: 0x3688128085cb9deca79dcac3e49e23825954fa17
  Linking ConvertLib to MetaCoin
  Deploying MetaCoin...
  ... 0x9f6a5f2b32cff09857b816ff5260f6a4cd503ebc92043334444071ea6c3fe490
  MetaCoin: 0x2947a78c0b5b45e0faa0b5593b5565437df0bb28
Saving successful migration to network...
  ... 0x5907e8729b89c7d5dce3e1c2c7f8f0e7a5cb67fa369ac2a9b9714d77255e1c7d
Saving artifacts...

E:\chp2>_
```

The preceding command helps create your contracts and conducts transactions for each of them. The following screenshot should help you clearly determine the factors that you need to look out for on your screen:

Here, you can observe the creation of the first contract post—some variables were updated and some transactions took place. The same process iterates to create multiple contracts each having their own variables and transactions.

Going back to your editor of choice, you will find these contracts in your `migration` folder. The process of deploying begins with the `migration` smart contract and then moves on to the `ConverLib` smart contract. `MetaCoin` is the last smart contract to be deployed. A more clear understanding can be achieved if we take a look at the `deploy_contracts.js` file that lies in the `migration` folder on your editor.

The following screenshot also helps you understand the order the smart contracts have been deployed in:

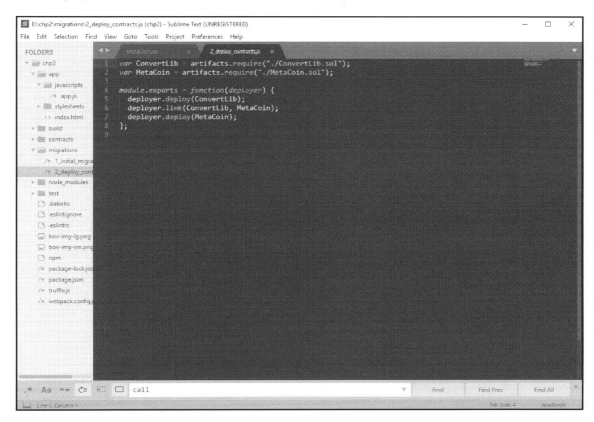

Exploring the Solidity syntax and JavaScript codes

This section will help us understand the Solidity syntax. We will explore the Solidity and JavaScript codes to understand our project in depth. This will also give us the power to alter the code to customize it to our needs.

Understanding the Solidity syntax

For understanding the syntax, let's take a look at the Solidity file `MetaCoin.sol`. The following screenshot will act as a guide so that we understand every line of code:

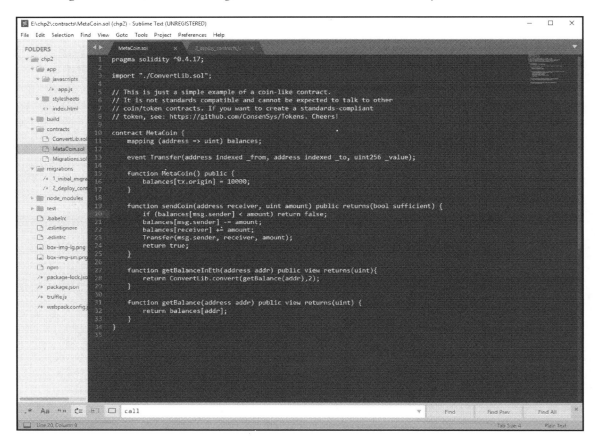

As you can see, every Solidity file begins with the definition of the Solidity version that you are currently using. In this case, that would be 0.4.17. This is immediately followed by the importing of the conversion library (commonly known as `ConvertLib.sol`). This is shown the the code block as follows:

```
pragma solidity ^0.4.17;

library ConvertLib{
    function convert(uint amount,uint conversionRate) public pure returns
(uint convertedAmount)
    {
```

```
        return amount * conversionRate;
    }
}
```

We will now move on to creating a contract. We will use the contract keyword followed by the name of your contract. For example, contract xyz. A contract runs is similar to the concept of a class in any other programming language:

```
contract MetaCoin {
```

The `MetaCoin` smart contract begins by adding the first variable that is mapping, a mapping called **balances**. Mapping is essentially a key value storage that allows you to map an address to an unsigned integer. This address can be a unique person or a unique account. This `mapping` function is the core variable of your application:

```
mapping (address => uint) balances;
```

The next variable that is defined is an event and it has three parameters assigned to it. These parameters are FROM, TO, and VALUE. An event can be used to trigger a JavaScript event or even to log some data:

```
event Transfer(address indexed _from, address indexed _to, uint256 _value);
```

The `MetaCoin` constructor is used to give the person who deployed the smart contracts 10,000 `MetaCoin`. This person is usually the administrator. It can also be another smart contract that has deployed this smart contract:

```
function MetaCoin() public {
    balances[tx.origin] = 10000;
}
```

The next function is `sendCoin`. It accepts two parameters: receiver and amount. It can also return a value. There are two methods to define a return value in a function. The first method would be a direct implementation of the return function, which is written as `returns(uint)`, and the second would be where we give it any name such as `returns(bool sufficient)`. This function uses the `if` loop to check if the sender of the message or the transaction has sufficient balance. The code then proceeds to check if the sender's balance is less than the amount he/she wants to send and, if it is, the value returned is false or an insufficient balance. If not, we just continue to move ahead and check that it deducts the amount from the sender and adds the same amount to the receiver.

```
function sendCoin(address receiver, uint amount) public returns(bool
sufficient) {
    if (balances[msg.sender] < amount) return false;
    balances[msg.sender] -= amount;
    balances[receiver] += amount;
```

```
    Transfer(msg.sender, receiver, amount);
    return true;
}
```

After this, the transfer event is triggered, which is followed by the log or the JavaScript event which will also return true to indicate that the sender did in fact have a sufficient balance:

```
function getBalanceInEth(address addr) public view returns(uint){
    return ConvertLib.convert(getBalance(addr),2);
}

function getBalance(address addr) public view returns(uint) {
    return balances[addr];
}
```

The `getBalanceInEth` and the `getBalance` functions are defined as views that return an integer. A view is a function that returns data for presenting. The `getBalanceInEth` function makes use of the Convert library and the first parameter that it passes is derived from the `getBalance` function. The `getBalance` function returns the balance of the parameter that is being passed. You can observe that `address.addr` is being externally called, hence it will be passed on the JavaScript side. The number two is passed as a second parameter. This is the conversion rate, whereas the first parameter is the amount. This is a simple multiplication to simulate a conversion between a token and ether.

We will now use `ConvertLib`, which is not only defined as a library but is also deployed separately. The following code helps us understand the workings a little better:

```
library ConvertLib{
    function convert(uint amount,uint conversionRate) public pure returns
(uint convertedAmount)
    {
        return amount * conversionRate;
    }
}
```

The primary benefit of this is that you can maintain a smart contract which contains your business logic and you can maintain a smart contract which contains a bunch of helper functions and maybe even variables.

Working with JavaScript

Truffle provides us with the tools to easily import and interface with our smart contracts. The following is a screenshot of a JavaScript code file named `app.js` which you can find in the `javascript` folder under the `app` directory:

The first import here is the `Web3` library which is by Ethereum. It interfaces with the Ethereum blockchain. It can request information or send a transaction based on the requirements of the moment.

The next import is the `truffle-contract`. It acts as a wrapper around the contract interface that Truffle provides.

We then proceed to import `metacoin_artifacts` from the `MetaCoin.JSON` file that lies in the `build` directory. A `MetaCoin` variable is initialized with this contract and we pass the `metacoin_artifacts` as a parameter to this contract constructor. This allows us to have a usable abstraction of the `MetaCoin` smart contract. The `MetaCoin` contract is used to set a provider and this provider is how we will interface with the blockchain.

The `currentProvider` is usually filled by whatever provides the `Web3` library, which in this case is `MetaMask`.

We then use the `Web3` library to get all of the accounts that are active within our setup of this test blockchain. The `getAccounts` function will get all of the accounts that are available on your installation which are actually owned by you. For understanding purposes, let's assume that each account represents multiple people or multiple accounts.

If you are running an actual, live blockchain node, the `getAccounts` function will not actually get all of the accounts in the concerned blockchain.

Once the accounts have been obtained, the `refreshBalance` function uses the `MetaCoin` abstraction that we defined earlier to get the deployed instances of the concerned contract. This instance is then used to get the balance. Keep in mind that this is not a transaction; this is a call that is used to get some data. Hence, the keyword call is used. A call won't actually cost us anything.

What would you change if this was actually a transaction? Not much. You would only eliminate the keyword `call`. Easy, right?

Let us proceed to define the first parameter of the `getBalance` function; the account parameter here coincides with the first parameter that we defined for the `getBalance` or the `getBalanceinEth` functions that belong to our Solidity file, `MetaCoin.sol`.

The second parameter here is some extra data that you can add to a call or a transaction. In this case, we can determine that it is from the same account that the call is for. After this is complete, we can either return a value or use this to update the `balance_element`. If an error occurs, it will get logged on the console.

A similar process is used for sending a coin—we again obtain the deployed instance and then use the `sendCoin` function. Looking closely will make us realize that there is no call keyword here as this is an actual transaction. A coin being sent from one person to another is a change in the blockchain, thus making this a transaction.

The further steps would remain the same; these include the syntax, the order of the parameters, and so on.

Bug fixing and debugging smart contracts

This section tells you how to go about bug fixing and debugging your code. Usually, the code will be debugged in the developer console which is similar to developing regular JavaScript code. If there is an error present in the JavaScript code, you could easily rectify it on the developer console. However, if the bug is in your smart contract, you are going to want to go a bit deeper. How are you going to debug your smart contract once it is live? Well, you cannot—not locally at least. What if somebody finds a bug? You need to find out where it came from. For these very reasons, we can use `remix.ethereum.org` and `etherscan.io`.

The modified version of the `MetaCoin Solidity` file found at `remix.ethereum.org` is as follows:

You can create this file yourself by clicking the little plus icon in the top-left corner and giving it a name of your choice. Once you compile this code, you will notice a green bar which indicates that the code has been compiled successfully. Let us try introducing an error by eliminating a semicolon; the bar will now turn red, indicating that there is some error that you need to rectify.

The following screenshot will help you understand the various tabs present on your screen:

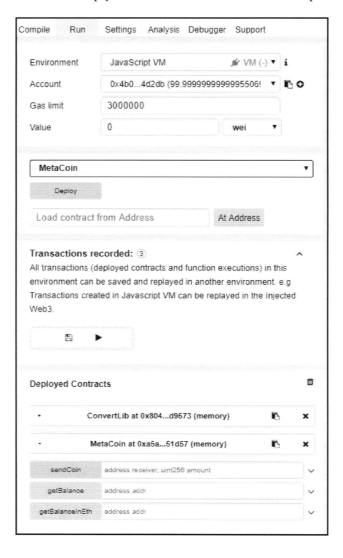

The **Run** tab encapsulates the Environment section, where we should make sure to select **JavaScript VM** as the environment that we wish to work on. This allows us to simulate the Ethereum blockchain within our browser, which is something similar to what TestRPC did.

You may notice that the constructor of the `MetaCoin Solidity` file now contains a `firstHolder` parameter. The `firstHolder` will be the first person to get 10,000 MetaCoins. You can vary the person who gets to be the `firstHolder`. You can select any account at random. You then need to make sure you copy it and give it as a parameter for the constructor. For addresses, it's usually a good idea to put them between quotes.

Upon creating a `MetaCoin`, the lower half of your screen will display a window that contains your transaction. It looks something as shown in the following screenshot:

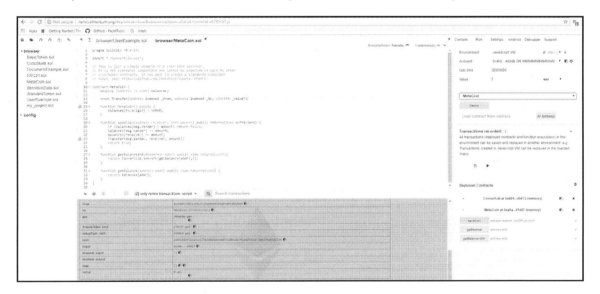

Transaction of coins

This window contains the details of the transaction. We can also debug the file. However, let us first get the balance of this person by copying the address to the **GetBalance** tab.

Once this is done, we can proceed to debug this. We can do it step by step to understand the process better. There will be only three steps as this is a small function.

Let us now try to send some coins between any two accounts. This will require us to copy the address of the second account and use it as a first parameter in the SendCoin tab. The second parameter of course will be the number of coins that you would like to transfer. Refer to the following screenshot for clarity:

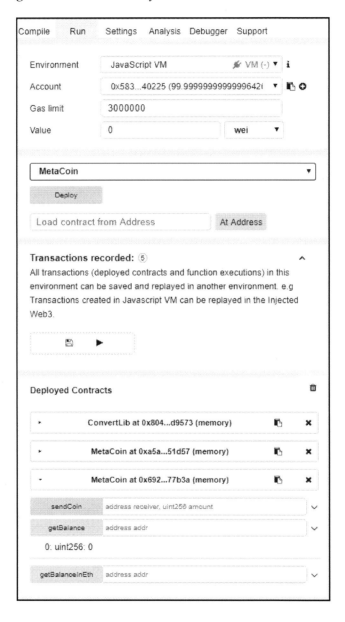

You can check the details of the transaction in the grey area under **Details** or **Debug** as shown in the following screenshot. You can also check the status of the transaction. To get a clear understanding, click debug to see the step-by-step process. Since remix is an open source project by the Ethereum developers, just about everyone and anyone can use it. You can use it locally by pulling it from Git or you can use it online. The choice is yours:

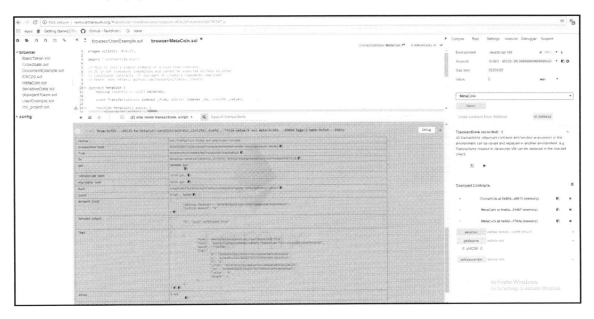

Getting the balance and send coins to different accounts

Once your smart contract is live, you can monitor transactions on etherscan.io. Just select any random transaction. You can see the source code or find out if it is a smart contract or not. The transaction information shows any transaction that has taken place. You can see the event logs, which display the text that is written by the events that you create in the Solidity codes. If any of these transactions have been done by you, you can trace them using Geth DebugTrace. If you try to trace any transaction that does not belong to you, you will encounter an error since there is not trace available. This can be seen in the tools and utilities section of the transaction.

The parity trace is just another Ethereum client that one can use. You will see the trace here, though it probably won't make a lot of sense. When your smart contract is live, you will not be fixing it—instead you will be updating it. You can always just debug it locally.

Changing our application with a better payment application

This section will focus on us improving our code. This will include adding functionalities such as depositing ether, gaining tokens, and withdrawing ether in exchange of tokens and also a creator fee.

We will work on the same code that was used for the previous section and continue to build on it.

As we do not want to give away free tokens in exchange for deposited ether, we will eliminate the following line of code completely:

```
function MetaCoin() public {
    balances[tx.origin] = 10000;
  }
```

We begin by setting a creator. To do this, we will need to define an address creator and a creatorFee as follows:

```
contract MetaCoin {
  mapping (address => uint) balances;
  address creator;
  uint creatorFee = 1;
  uint collectedFees = 0;
  uint conversionRate = 5;

  uint CURRENCY_MULTIPLIER = 10**18;
```

The collectedFees is what one might call a pot. This is used to collect the creatorFees. The conversion rate is the rate that is used to multiply the number of tokens. For example, if you have one ether, you will get five tokens in exchange. Let us consider that one has 0.1 ether; the conversion still works with integers at the backend. The currency_multiplier is used to equate the values of your tokens and ether. The smallest denomination is a wei.

We also need to initialize the creator as the message.sender when the smart contract is being created:

```
function MetaCoin() public {
    creator = msg.sender;
  }
```

The creator needs some special functions of its own, such as one for the withdrawal of fees. This requires us to create a modifier called `onlyCreator`. It would look something as follows in the code here:

```
modifier onlyCreator() {
        if (msg.sender == creator || tx.origin ==creator) {
            _;
        }
}
```

This adds the condition that if the `message.sender` is the creator or if the `transaction.origin` comes from the creator, only then will the code be executed. This is done by adding an underscore.

The next step would be to create a function called `collectFees`. For the code's sake, we'll make it public, but such that only the creator can call this function. Your code should look something as follows:

```
function collectFees() public onlyCreator {
        creator.transfer(collectedFees);
        collectedFees = 0;
}
```

Now we will transfer the funds to the creator and set the collectedFees to 0. Now, what we do want to add is some functions so that whenever somebody sends a coin, we want a part of that coin to be able to go to the creator, and for this we will create the deposit and the withdraw functions.

The deposit function will be a payable function. A payable function is used whenever you want to receive ether. If you do forget to use it, it will just display an error:

```
function depsoit() public payable {
        balances[msg.sender] += msg.value * conversionRate *
            CURRENCY_MULTIPLIER;
}
```

The conversion rate used has already been set in the contract function. Remember, our tokens will work the same as one ether; that means one token will be multiplied by 10 to the power 18. So when you deposit any tokens, it will be multiplied by the `CURRENCY_MULTIPLIER`.

We will then move on to the withdraw function. There has to be some amount of caution while implementing this, because we first need to multiply with a currency multiplier that has been set in the contract function. Then we will proceed to deduct the balance of the executor of the transaction with the amount that needs to be withdrawn. The amount will be divided by the conversion rate. The code for this is as follows:

```
function withdraw(uint amount) public {
        amount = amount * CURRENCY_MULTIPLIER;
        balances[msg.sender] -= amount;
        msg.sender.transfer(amount / conversionRate);
    }
```

Summary

In this chapter, we took a look at how to create an Ethereum based application. We also deployed and tested the same projects. We then delved into the Solidity syntax which isn't only vast but is also extensive. JavaScript codes were also looked into. We learned how to fix bugs using our own systems as well as externally. In the end, we finally converted our project into a payment application.

The next chapter focuses on the concepts of creating our own tokens. We will take closer look at ICO's and also at handling our own token transactions.

3
Creating Your Own Cryptocurrency on the Ethereum Blockchain

In this chapter, we are going to have a look at how we can create our own ERC20 token project. An ERC20 token is a cryptocurrency built on top of the Ethereum blockchain. We will have a look at its specifications, and how you can do an initial coin offering. We will also learn how to handle token transactions and transfer value.

The topics that we'll be covering in this chapter are as follows:

- Creating a cryptocurrency/ERC20 token project
- ERC20 standard/specification
- Initial coin offerings
- Handling token transactions

Creating an ERC20 token

In this section, you will learn how to create an ERC20 token. We will start by setting up a new project—we are going to use the OpenZeppelin Solidity framework to create our project.

Installing OpenZepplin Solidity

OpenZeppelin is basically just a collection of smart contracts that you can import into your own smart contracts in order to speed up your development. They can also make your smart contracts much more secure from the get-go.

You can visit the OpenZeppelin GitHub page at `OpenZeppelin Github`:

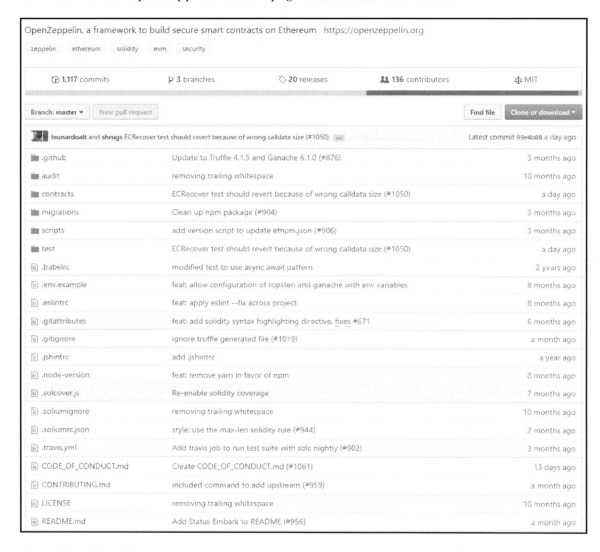

If you have been browsing through the Truffle website—`truffleframework.com`—then you have probably come across **Ganache**. We will be using it throughout this section. **Ganache** is a GUI that is basically easier to navigate with than TestRPC, but while doing all the same things as TestRPC. You can download it for Windows or any other OS if you go to Ganache's GitHub page at `Ganache GitHub`.

The `ethereumjs-testrpc` has been deprecated and it has been renamed to `ganache-cli`. For detailed information you can visit the following link: `https://www.npmjs.com/package/ethereumjs-testrpc`.

After downloading it, you can run it. Upon opening the application, you will see a UI similar to the following screenshot:

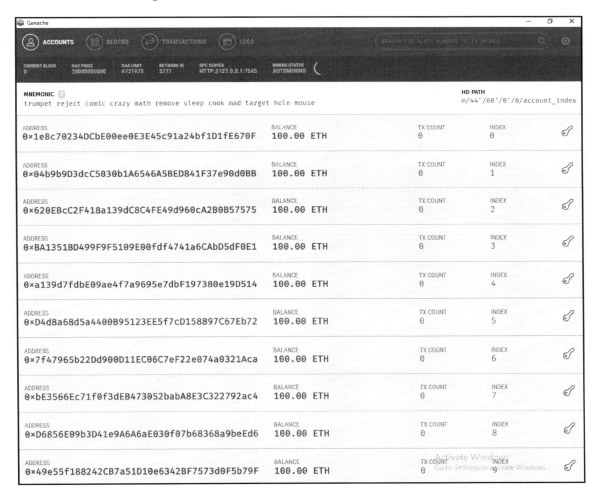

Ganache

This should be familiar: These are your 10 accounts that are generated by TestRPC. You can see your blocks, your transactions, and your logs.

Setting up new project

To set up a new project, go through the following steps:

1. Create a new folder for the project.
2. On the console, run the truffle command, `truffle -cli unbox webpack`.

```
E:\chp3>truffle-cli unbox webpack
Downloading...
Unpacking...
Setting up...
Unbox successful. Sweet!

Commands:

  Compile:              truffle compile
  Migrate:              truffle migrate
  Test contracts:       truffle test
  Run linter:           npm run lint
  Run dev server:       npm run dev
  Build for production: npm run build

E:\chp3>_
```

3. Run the `npm install -E` command. Because OpenZeppelin recommends specifying `-E` and will pull a specific version of OpenZeppelin, it will never update it, and will keep the same version. This is because it doesn't have semantic versioning yet.
4. Run `npm install -E zeppelin-solidity`. OpenZeppelin is a lot more secure because it has been built with security in mind from the very start.
5. Let's switch over to the editor now. Here, we will find our starter project.

6. Lets start by removing things that we don't need. Under **migrations**, click on `deploy contracts` and remove the deployment of the `ConvertLib` by deleting the `ConvertLib` variable and the `deployer.deploy()` variable; allow to `deployer.link()` keep the `MetaCoin` variable:

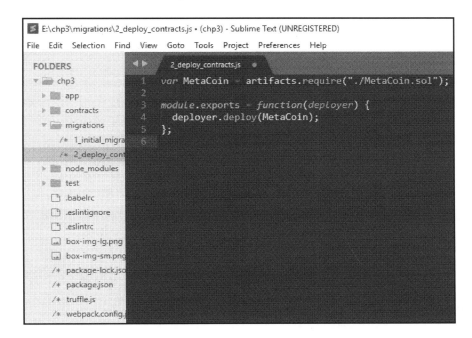

7. Go into the `contracts` folder and delete `ConvertLib.sol` by right-clicking on it and then clicking **Delete File**.
8. In the `MetaCoin Solidity` file, remove `ConvertLib`. Remove all of the function code.

9. Import the standard token from OpenZeppelin. OpenZeppelin is a basic ERC20 interface that we can use by running the command `import 'zeppelin-solidity/contracts/tokens/ERC20/StandardToken.sol';`. This imports the `StandardToken` Solidity file from the OpenZeppelin framework, and it knows to look inside of your `node modules` folder:

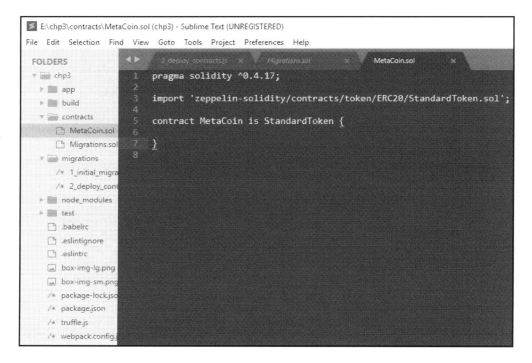

10. We can now define MetaCoin for this. Ahead of `contract MetaCoin` add `is StandardToken`.

11. Now let's migrate MetaCoin. Make sure that Ganache is running. Under **RPC server**, you should see that Ganache runs on localhost or port number `7545`. Truffle by default runs on `7545`; you should be able to see this in the editor:

12. Now, to migrate the `MetaCoin`, we can run the `truffle -cli migrate` command:

```
E:\chp3>truffle-cli migrate
Compiling .\contracts\MetaCoin.sol...
Compiling zeppelin-solidity/contracts/token/ERC20/StandardToken.sol...
Compiling zeppelin-solidity\contracts\math\SafeMath.sol...
Compiling zeppelin-solidity\contracts\token\ERC20\BasicToken.sol...
Compiling zeppelin-solidity\contracts\token\ERC20\ERC20.sol...
Compiling zeppelin-solidity\contracts\token\ERC20\ERC20Basic.sol...
Writing artifacts to .\build\contracts

Using network 'development'.

Running migration: 2_deploy_contracts.js
  Deploying MetaCoin...
  ... 0x4e7e12ad452a3836f2f16881d5adf5c518fa1778cd6f0dd4f4d5e3199bf83f24
  MetaCoin: 0xb53fef326f9ef4b72dce78a88bc2cb9e0b14825f
Saving successful migration to network...
  ... 0x94d530561588fdbd5476a9a3a720493c7a530ac80f3725c9808f6bf9149a6b9d
Saving artifacts...
```

13. You should now see that it's compiling your MetaCoin, migrations, and also a lot of files from the OpenZeppelin framework.

After performing all of these steps, our Ganache should look something similar to the following:

Ganache after making contract calls

You should now see that your transactions have gone through. Ganache has made a contract call, creating contracts. We are all set to proceed further.

Deploying and testing ERC20 tokens

In this section, we will have a look at how we can deploy and test our ERC20 token, or cryptocurrency. We will have a look at some of the pitfalls and security concerns that you may encounter when you are transferring tokens, and we will look at the Solidity and JavaScript that will be required to transfer those tokens. We will also be testing them out using Ganache and MetaMask.

Deploying ERC20 tokens

First of all, we need some data to enter into the editor. In the `MetaCoin.sol`, we need to define a name, a symbol, the number of decimal places, and `INITIAL_SUPPLY`. We will also assign our `INITIAL_SUPPLY` to the `totalSupply` in the constructor. We will also give the creator of the token the `INITIAL_SUPPLY`.

We know that we need `totalSupply` because if you go to `StandardToken`, found under `node modules | zeppelin-solidity | contracts | token | ERC20 | StandardToken`, then you can see that this imports `ERC20` and `BasicToken`. Now, if we go to the `ERC20` folder, we can see that this is an interface, but `BasicToken.sol` implements this interface. So let's go to the `BasicToken.sol` folder. It will have `totalSupply`, `balances`. I hope you remember this from the last chapter. It has a `Transfer` function that makes use of `SafeMath` from the `SafeMath.Solidity` file. This a little Solidity file that will make sure that whenever you perform a mathematical operation, your input and your output data will be correct, and that it won't corrupt anything, because once data is inside the blockchain, it stays in the blockchain. So, after defining this, we can just go ahead and deploy it. Go through the following steps to deploy the ERC20 tokens, your first cryptocurrency:

1. Let's make sure that Ganache is running.
2. Once Ganache is running, copy the mnemonic and paste it in the `metamask.io` **Restore Vault**. We have done this before, as you might remember.

You can even reinstall MetaMask to reset everything. This makes it simpler, as MetaMask doesn't have this functionality yet.

3. Press **OK**. You should see nothing, initially. Check for the network. If you are on your main network, you will have to connect to `http://localhost:7545`—this is the port that Ganache is listening on. You can do this by clicking the drop-down arrow beside the main network and selecting `Custom RPC`. Type in the localhost URL mentioned previously and click **Save**. You should see that MetaMask has instantly connected. You can have a look at your account; you should have some ether:

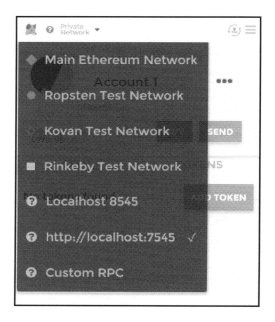

4. Go to the `migrations` folder and make sure that it has `var MetaCoin`.
5. Let's go to `MetaCoin.sol`. Note that the `INITIAL_SUPPLY` will divided by the amount of decimals specified.
6. Switch to the terminal window. Type the `truffle-cli migrate` command. You should be able to see the transactions that have come up successfully. Copy the contract token:

```
E:\chp3>truffle-cli migrate
Using network 'development'.

Running migration: 1_initial_migration.js
  Deploying Migrations...
  ... 0xb60980748020609c66540dbc20e849072b6ae2424c5e3bad783309ab9903215a
  Migrations: 0x5dfba046aeb3ed90848030d2490cc5d291106c48
Saving successful migration to network...
  ... 0x8bc5118ca888e23515d7016dd5c28b82b4bf9811638974aba0423c44d28c760c
Saving artifacts...
Running migration: 2_deploy_contracts.js
  Deploying MetaCoin...
  ... 0xc3d1f13316587a5d112081c2bd73411f75607315aae526bcf194908e96f64f66
  MetaCoin: 0xb53fef326f9ef4b72dce78a88bc2cb9e0b14825f
Saving successful migration to network...
  ... 0x94d530561588fdbd5476a9a3a720493c7a530ac80f3725c9808f6bf9149a6b9d
Saving artifacts...
```

Contract token

7. After copying this, you can head over to MetaMask. Access the top-left icon, click on `Add Token`, and paste the token address in the token address section. It will automatically retrieve the token symbol and the specified number of decimals. Click on **Add**. You will see your first tokens, preceded by your symbol:

8. Now you can create an account by clicking the user icon above. You will now have a second account. Get out of the token tab and you will see that you have 0 tokens on the second account:

9. Now, there is a little surprise here. You can just use the code you already had to send these tokens over. The difference between the MetaCoin from the last example and this one is that now the tokens are actually following a real standard, namely, the ERC20 standard. It states that you need a name, a token symbol, decimals, and an `INITIAL_SUPPLY`.

10. To transfer tokens run, the `npm run dev` commands.

11. Open the web browser and navigate to `localhost:8080`:

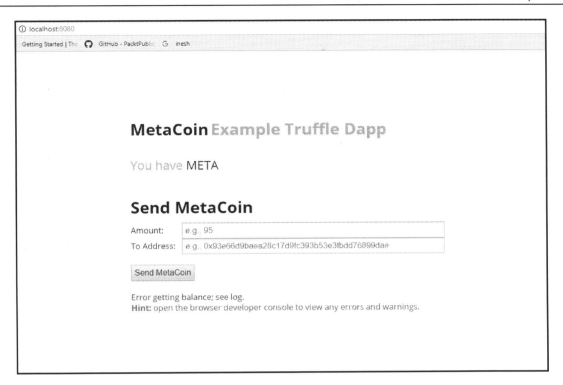

12. Go to the editor. The JavaScript function will still try to call the getBalance function, but this has been changed. You can see this if you go to the BasicToken Solidity file; you will see that you have balanceOf. So let's go to the app | JavaScripts | app.js and then on to the refreshBalance function. Here, we change the meta.getBalance to meta.balanceOf. Also, go to the sendCoin function and change meta.sendCoin to meta.transfer. Make sure that you have the same kind of method signature in BasicToken.sol under the ERC20 folder:

```
var meta;
MetaCoin.deployed().then(function(instance) {
  meta = instance;
  return meta.balanceOf.call(account, {from: account});
}).then(function(value) {
  var balance_element = document.getElementById("balance");
  balance_element.innerHTML = value.valueOf();
}).catch(function(e) {
  console.log(e);
  self.setStatus("Error getting balance; see log.");
});
},
```

13. Now go to the browser on the `localhost:8080` page. Switch to the first account. There it is. You won't see the decimals in place, but that is just a frontend stuff; we will look into that later:

Testing ERC20 tokens

We will now test on your second account.

1. Copy the address of your second account, as shown in the following screenshot:

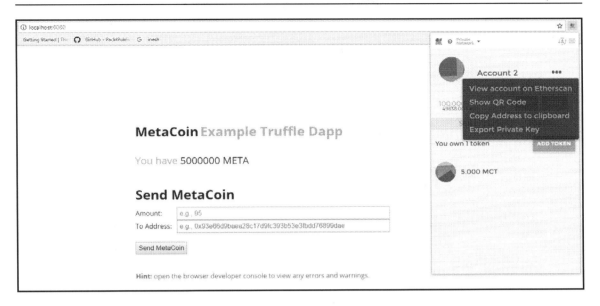

Copying the address of the second account

2. You need to make the change in the `app.js` file in the `javascript` folder under the `app` directory of your project:

```
var meta;
MetaCoin.deployed().then(function(instance) {
  meta = instance;
  return meta.transfer(receiver, amount, {from: account});
}).then(function() {
  self.setStatus("Transaction complete!");
  self.refreshBalance();
}).catch(function(e) {
  console.log(e);
  self.setStatus("Error sending coin; see log.");
});
}
```

3. Switch to the first account and send your **MetaCoin**. Put in a value, such as 5,000,000 units (equal to 5 tokens). This value should be less than the value specified in the `INITIAL_SUPPLY`. Remember that `INITIAL_SUPPLY` divided by the decimals will give 5 tokens, hence 5,000,000. Paste the address and click **Send MetaCoin**:

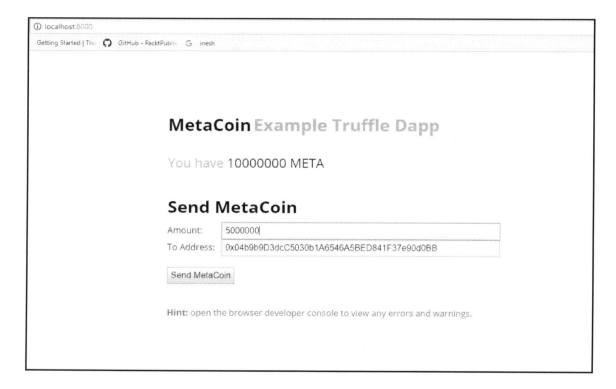

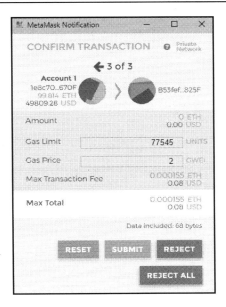

4. On refreshing the page, you will see that both of your accounts will have tokens:

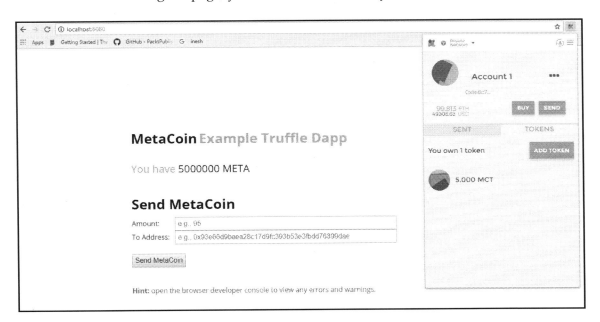

You have now created your first ERC20 standard cryptocurrency and deployed it.

Understanding token standards

In this section, we will have a deeper look into ERC20 tokens and why there was a need for other token standards, such as ERC721 and ERC827.

ERC20

If you go to `Ethereum wiki` and have a look at the ERC20 token standards, you can see all the functions and events that you can implement. Moreover, most tokens are ERC20 compliant. You can see that the **Golem network token** (**GNT**) is only partially ERC20 compliant, but it is still a standard token; you don't exactly have to follow everything, but it is always better if you do. Among these functions, what we haven't seen before is `allowance` and `approve`. These functions can be useful in certain situations. If, for example, you have 20 MetaCoin tokens, you can say *I want my friend or another account to spend tokens in my name*. Well, you can do this with the `approve` function. With the `allowance` function, you can specify a spender and how many tokens you want them to be able to spend.

ERC721

Lets move on to `EIP GitHub`. EIP stands for Ethereum Improvement Protocol. Here, in the **Issues** tab, we can see a lot of discussions about improvements. If you feel that you can suggest an improvement, you can write it in a draft. It was through such discussions that somebody came up with `ERC: Non-Fungible Token Standard`.

First, let's define what a fungible token is. By definition, a fungible token is spendable for a set amount of goods or services or other tradeable items. In a similar manner, a dollar can be spent or a dollar can be traded for a euro. in that respect, non-fungible tokens are more like baseball cards, where you can have two of either can quote or unquote options on the same card, but one can have more value than the other because of the value that people attach to it. This is the case with ERC721 tokens. If you go to `ERC-721 definition`, you can see a brief definition. You can see the `name()`, `symbol()`, and `totalsupply()`.

In this definition, you can have a token, and a token has an owner; you don't have to give the token to the owner, you can just trade it. The token also has metadata, and this metadata specifies which properties a token has, which then means that it has a value. So this very much makes these tokens like baseball cards, or, if you're familiar with them, Ethereum CryptoKitties:

CryptoKitties is an example of this kind of token. It is a collectible, breedable, and adorable kind of token. Visit `cryptokitties.co` for more information. At their marketplace, you can see CryptoKitties for sale. Some are being sold by people like you and me for ethers, as shown in the following screenshot:

CryptoKitties Marketplace

Some of them are even exclusive CryptoKitties. They are really special tokens sold for a high number of ethers.

You can trade these CryptoKitties for ether, and the price will always vary according to what you want to set. These are some of my kitties:

New Arrivals

No more than 50,000 Gen 0s will ever be created! Collect the latest traits and unlock the newest mewtations by adding one to your collection. A new Gen 0 is born every 15 minutes... until the end of November 2018!

 For sale Ξ 0.0908

 For sale Ξ 0.0899

 For sale Ξ 0.089

 For sale Ξ 0.0881

Kitty 849219   Kitty 849212   Kitty 849201   Kitty 849187

Browse All

Fancy Cats

All of these Kitties come with custom art, which makes them rare (and adorable).

 For sale Ξ 0.3963

 For sale Ξ 0.1274

 For sale Ξ 0.5

 For sale Ξ 0.1

Kitty 848017 · Gen 7 · Snappy   **Kitty 843038** · Gen 7 · Snappy   **Kitty 829969** · Gen 9 · Snappy   **Kitty 821093** · Gen 8 · Snappy

My kitties

ERC827

Again, if you visit EIP GitHub, you will get an abstract, and an explanation as to why we need the ERC827 token standard. You can actually specify some data or a function that you want to be executed once a transfer has taken place. This can be done using the following function:

```
function transferAndCall(address _to, uint256 _value, bytes _data) public
payable returns (bool) {
    require(_to != address(this));
    require(super.transfer(_to, _value));
    require(_to.call(_data));
    return true;
}
```

 You can find this function following link: https://github.com/ethereum/
EIPs/issues/827.

You call the preceding function on the address of the receiver.

This is all about the token standards. This is not the end—a lot of new token standards will surely be coming in the future. There are certainly a lot of proposals. Not all of them get accepted, but when they do, that is because they really bring something new to the table. You can even go ahead and place an improvement; who knows, it may turn out to be a new token standard! Now we can learn how to use our tokens to pay for the execution of some logic for a smart contract.

Using tokens and executing logic

You might be wondering how a third person could execute a call upon receiving tokens. Actually, it is ridiculously easy. This can be done in JavaScript using the Web3 library provided by Ethereum. The following is a smart contract shown on remix. We have explored remix earlier:

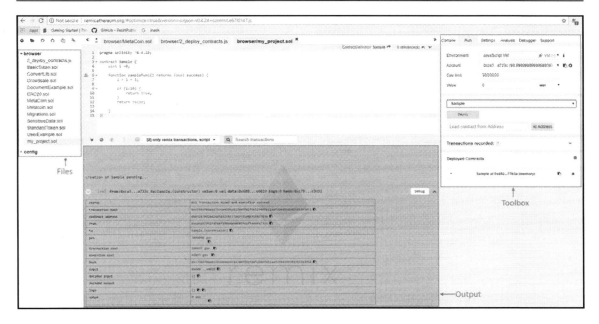

A smart contract

This just increments an integer, checks whether it's less than 10, and returns true if it is; it returns false otherwise. You can just use **JavaScript VM** for this problem. On compiling and running, if you click the `SampleFunc`, there will be a new entry added in the gray area. If you click on **Details**, you will see an input entry—you can copy this. This will be your third parameter for this function. You can execute this like any other function.

Now, if you send tokens using the ERC827 smart contract, this function will be executed.

But what is the use of this? In a word, security. A recipient can withdraw tokens, quote or unquote, and receive them. The reason for this the operation that in a smart contract, you don't want to just send tokens and assume that it has been successful. Assuming success like this has led to some pretty big hacks in the past. What you can do is go for some kind of withdrawal scheme where you send tokens and then make them available for withdrawal by the recipient.

Summary

In this chapter, we learned how to create ERC20 tokens, and then deploy and test them. We also looked at different token standards, saw some examples of tokens, such as CryptoKitties, and saw the scope of new standards that may come in the future. We also learned how to use these tokens and execute logic when someone receives these tokens. In the next chapter, we will learn how to sign documents and work with bigger files, and then build an application using this knowledge!

4

Signing Legal Documents on Blockchains and Identity Verification

The vast usage of blockchains necessitates a chapter dedicated to the topic. The versatility that blockchains have tempts users to try their hand at implementing them in the various areas of our lives. Though sometimes it might seems tedious, using decentralized ledgers to store and handle data is actually very convenient and safe, to a certain extent. Accessing these ledgers over a network to perform activities such as transactions or signing documents makes it a feasible method of conveying data without actually doing much.

This chapter will focus on the following topics:

- User identity and storing sensitive data on a blockchain
- Dealing with large files on a blockchain
- User identity verification on a blockchain
- Signing a document on a blockchain

This chapter is more theoretical than some of the others as a lot of it depends on the backend technologies that we choose to work on.

User identity and sensitive data on the blockchain

Let us begin by discussing the prime aspect for user identity—the parameter that is used for verification. We can do this by using a person's email address, their phone number, or even a physical address. One might wonder how we can do this. It is actually very easy to verify any of the aforementioned parameters on the blockchain. To do this, we can use a confirmation code. The user can link this confirmation code to their Ethereum account, which in turn links it to his/her private key. As an administrator, you have to make sure that it is not you who generates this code. This would give you the power to fabricate users at will. You want your users to be real and verified people to eradicate the trustless element from your blockchain. To generate these codes, we can use Twilio or any external service provider. Twilio is used extensively for SMS verification, which encapsulates phone verification.

Let's now consider the case of dealing with sensitive data, which cannot be stored on public blockchains. You might think to yourself, *There are private blockchains*. I know, I know. But for now, assume that all blockchains are public blockchains. You cannot store sensitive data such as your name, phone number, or email address on this particular blockchain. This would be a huge privacy concern. One of the things that is necessary for a successful blockchain is genuine proof that validates the fact that data stored on it cannot be tampered with. This involves not keeping the entire blockchain on the centralized server. To solve this, we will resort to hashing and using our backend storage including MySQL or Oracle.

Hashing

Hashing is a method that transforms a large string value to a small, fixed-length value. It is used for the purpose of indexing. Searching for a string is difficult as compared to a value. Hashing not only makes indexing easier but also affects the search time for any string. It reduces the search time, as finding a short value is much easier and more efficient as compared to the original string value.

To learn how to perform hashing, you will begin by hashing some user information and storing this in your smart contract, thus allowing you to link an anonymous blockchain identity to a real-life identity.

For this to work, you need to encourage your user to create a new Ethereum account for your application. This will provide them with anonymity when they use this account outside your application.

Using private blockchains is also a solution. The drawbacks of this outweigh its advantages. Two of these drawbacks concern data tampering and data censoring. However, these concerns turn into issues only if the blockchain is hosted by entities under your control. Finding a way around these issues is something that banks are currently interested in. Let us assume we have banks A, B, and C. These three banks have teamed up together to use one single private blockchain, irrespective of the fact that they are in competition with each other. This leads to them developing internal security measures that make it impossible for anyone to manipulate the data.

To understand this better, let us look at an example that involves us verifying the identity of a user. This begins with the user accessing your application and generating a new address and a new private key. He could also use MetaMask, Geth, or any other provider to do this. The backend system would notify the smart contract of a new and unverified user, and the third-party application, such as Twilio, would send out a verification code. At this point, even though you are an admin, you will not be able to see the code. This prevents the possibility of users being fabricated out of thin air by any member of the administrative team. Once the code has been entered, it will be passed to the smart contract.

```
pragma solidity ^0.4.17;

contract SensitiveDataExample {
  bytes32[] userHashes;
  // The backend would take a user-object. For example a simple JSON
  // {name: "Kenny", familyName: "Vaneetvelde", address: "Some Address
123"}
  // After hashing this entire object, you can pass it to the function
below.
  // Later, you can re-hash it, to verify the user and data if/when needed.
  function addUser(bytes32 userHash) {
    userHashes.push(userHash);
  }
}
```

The preceding code is a JSON file that will show us how to use hashing to protect sensitive data by hashing it:

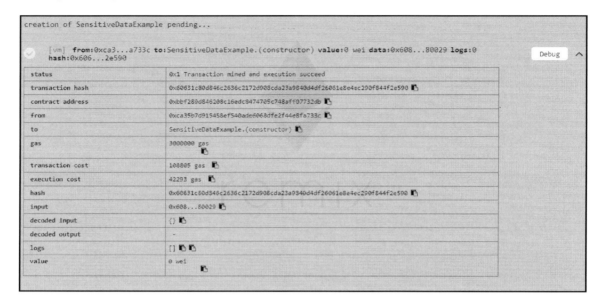

SensitiveData.sol file on remix.org with output

The data here is hashed and then passed to the `addUser` function. This will allow the data to remain within your own database.

If you try to manipulate data as an evil administrator, your hash would not be right. Once the hash is passed to the `addUser` function, the `addUser` function will push the `userHash` on top of the `userHashes` array of bytes.

Dealing with files and large data on the blockchain

In this section, we are going to learn how to deal with large files and documents on any blockchain. As mentioned umpteen times before, blockchains are usually public in nature, and therefore, privacy and security should be of prime importance. A blockchain contains all of the data that is filled into it, which in the case of Ethereum causes the cost to increase—that is, more gas is paid per transaction. As this isn't something that we want, we'll use a few workarounds.

One of these workaround is **Swarm**. There is also IPFS, or the InterPlanetary File System, which we learned about briefly in `Chapter 1`, *Workflow Setup and Thinking Blockchain*. You could also use your own server to store the data and larger files.

Swarm and IPFS are not blockchains, but they do follow the common principles of decentralization, making the two of them decentralized file-storage systems that are tamperproof.

A file is not decentralized in the beginning. When a file is uploaded through IPFS, you become the first, sole host of that file. The moment someone else downloads or requests the same file, they also become a host, and the rest of the network has a reference to who the hosts are. This connectivity between the peers allows a person to download or query a file by redirecting you to the right location/person.

Since Swarm and IPFS are not completely developed, you can opt to use your own systems and some hashing. You would start by making a SHA hash file in your backend and storing this file in a blockchain. This file can no longer be edited without changing the hash, thereby invalidating the hash.

In any scenario, if a user wants to validate their contract, they just rehash the file to compare it to the original hash. This acts as an assurance that their contract hasn't been tampered with.

Let us look at the following code example that will help us understand the concept of hashing in a bit more depth:

```solidity
pragma solidity ^0.4.17;

contract DocumentExample {
  bytes32[] documentHashes;

  function addDocument(bytes32 documentHash) {
    documentHashes.push(documentHash);
  }
}
```

The output for the preceding code in remix:

In the preceding screenshot, we have hashed the entire document, and we will also add that hash to the smart contract or to the blockchain by calling the `addDocument` function, which will pass the hash and push it onto the array.

User identity verification with blockchains

This section takes a closer look at the user verification process and the Solidity code that lies behind it. Let us consider the following Solidity code:

```solidity
pragma solidity ^0.4.17;
contract UserExample {

  mapping(address => bool) user_verified;
  mapping(address => bytes32) user_codes;

  mapping(bytes32 => address) to_sign;
  mapping(bytes32 => bool) signed;

  address owner;

  modifier onlyOwner() {
  require(msg.sender == owner);
  _;
```

```
}

function UserExample() public {
owner = msg.sender;
}

function addUser(address user, bytes32 hashed_verification) public
onlyOwner {
user_verified[user] = false;
user_codes[user] = hashed_verification;
}

function verify(bytes32 verification_code) public {
if (user_verified[msg.sender] == false &&
sha256(verification_code) == user_codes[msg.sender]) {
user_verified[msg.sender] = true;
}
}
}
```

As you can see, the owner is your own server. The constructor defines the value of the owner as `message.sender`, which contains the address of the person who deploys the smart contract.

The following are the steps that the code goes through:

1. A user accesses your application.
2. The same user enters some private details.
3. Details are stored in the form of a hash in the smart contract of choice.
4. Twilio or a third-party service provider will send a text message to the user while the system calls the Solidity function named `add.User`.
5. The `add.User` function passes two parameters, namely, `address user` and a `hashed_verification`, which is an array of 32 bytes and contains your hash of the code that has been sent to the user. This function can be called only by the owner or the modifier, which in this case is you or your server.
6. The contract constructor consists of a Boolean value that stores the address that is mapped by the `user_verified` that lies in the `add.User` function. This Boolean value defaults to the `false` value.
7. The `user_codes` maps `hashed_verification` to an array of 32 bytes.
8. The user enters the code on your frontend.

9. The `verify` function then checks whether or not the user is verified by comparing the hash of the verification code that the user has provided with the hash that is sent by the admin in the `add.User` function.

 You don't hash the verification code in JavaScript for future verification because third parties can just take this code, hash it, and check it.

10. Once the user is verified, the default Boolean value is changed from `false` to `true`.
11. The verification code is then stored in plain text on the blockchain after the user is verified.

Signing a document on the blockchain

This section will teach you how to sign documents such as contracts on the blockchain. Let us consider the following code to understand how this is done:

```
pragma solidity ^0.4.17;
contract UserExample {

mapping(address => bool) user_verified;
mapping(address => bytes32) user_codes;

mapping(bytes32 => address) to_sign;
mapping(bytes32 => bool) signed;

address owner;

modifier onlyOwner() {
require(msg.sender == owner);
_;
}

function UserExample() public {
owner = msg.sender;
}

function inviteUser(bytes32 documentHash, address user) public onlyOwner {
to_sign[documentHash] = user;
}
```

```
function signDocument(bytes32 documentHash) public {
if (msg.sender != to_sign[documentHash]) {
revert();
}
signed[documentHash] = true;
}
function addUser(address user, bytes32 hashed_verification) public
onlyOwner {
user_verified[user] = false;
user_codes[user] = hashed_verification;
}

function verify(bytes32 verification_code) public {
if (user_verified[msg.sender] == false &&
sha256(verification_code) == user_codes[msg.sender]) {
user_verified[msg.sender] = true;
}
}
}
```

The following screenshot is the result of the preceding code in the remix–Solidity framework:

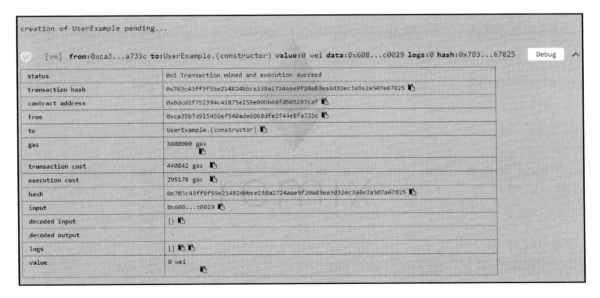

Output of the UserExample.sol file in remix

This code allows you to add a user to your blockchain. It also allows you to invite and allow the user to sign a document. Since the code is similar to the one we used in the previous section, entitled *User identity verification with blockchains*, we will only take a look at the amendments we have made to the code to accommodate the extra feature—namely, allowing the user to sign a contract.

If we look at the code closely, we will notice that there are two new parameter mappings. One maps a 32-byte array (bytes32) to an address that is a user, while the other one maps a 32-byte array (bytes32) to a Boolean called signed.

Structs can also be used to map variables.

Once the contract is deployed, you can upload a document, hash it, and then proceed to add it to the blockchain. Once this is done, you can invite a user. Inviting a user leads to the user being added to the to_sign mapping at the documentHash. Let us assume that we have something like the following code:

```
//to_sign[0x121212121212] = 0x121212133293928
```

Here, 0x121212121212 is the hash and 0x121212133293928 is your user. You could then notify the user regarding his invitation via an email that contains a link to the document. The user can use this link to view and verify this document. The process of verification on the user end would require them to hash the document and then compare it to the hash that was provided to them. In the event that the user wants to take the process of verification a bit further, they can look the hash up on the blockchain itself. After this, the user can call the signDocument function.

To understand how the signDocument function works, let us assume that you want to sign the 0x1212 hash. You should first call the function with the first parameter as the user. First, it will check whether your address is different from the address of the invited user. If this is true, your transaction will be canceled using the revert function, which in this code is null. If the two addresses match, we can simply proceed to sign the document.

This is one of the reasons I love blockchains. One can simply sign a document by setting a variable to true. Once this variable has been set to true, you can regard this document as signed. If this is used as evidence in court, the document should hold, as it has been signed with a private key. This makes it undeniable that the person has signed the contract knowingly.

Summary

This chapter took us on a journey where we learned how to handle large data files on a blockchain. Given that data sensitivity is a concept that is a necessity given the current developments in the World, we learned some simple methods to implement the security of a blockchain. We then learned about the process of verifying the identity of a real-world user on a blockchain with the help of third parties, and learned how to sign a document with the help of a blockchain.

The next chapter will teach us the basic concepts and methods required to use Ethereum outside our browsers, and also how it is used as the backbone of the IoT. We will also take a quick glance at the physical components that make up a blockchain.

Ethereum Outside the PC/Web Environment

So far, we've looked at using Ethereum on your own personal computers. This chapter takes a look at the uses of Ethereum in various other applications: smartphones, being the most commonly use electronic device, are one of them. The current growth of technology demands an automatic system that requires us to implement the **Internet of Things (IoT)**. This chapter focuses on the following topics:

- Ethereum outside the browser
- Ethereum and IoT
- Ethereum and smartphone applications
- Further steps and resources

We are going to have a look at how people use Ethereum outside the browser, how people use Ethereum as the backbone of IoT, and how you can work with physical components in the blockchain. In addition, we will have a look at how you can use Ethereum in smartphone applications. We'll also discuss some further steps and resources that you can use. So let's get started by looking at how you can use Ethereum outside the browser.

Ethereum outside the browser

This section will teach us to work with Ethereum outside the browser. Standard libraries that can be used on Java, Python, Go, or .NET have been developed by the Ethereum team. These are accessible directly from GitHub at `https://github.com/ethereum`.

One essential feature that you need in order to use Ethereum outside your browser is a connection to the Ethereum network. This connection can be direct—that is, connected directly to your application—or you can use a relay server. Even though using a relay server is not an optimal option, it is completely possible. To use a relay server, you first need to have a server of your own that is centralized in nature and only accepts presigned transactions.

Another requirement that is necessary for using Ethereum outside your browser is the Ethereum library of the language that you will be using to develop it. This is optional because we always start any transaction with raw data. To get a transaction going on the Ethereum network, we need to encode the raw data and assign a private key to it. The transaction is protected from modification because it is signed with a private key. After this, you can send it to the network. This can be done with the help of a relay server. There is some selective muting that takes place, and hence it is a more reliable option to make sure that you send the transactions to the networks by yourself. The following links can be used to do this, depending upon the software that you are using:

- If you are a Python user, the `Web3.py` library can be used. It is freely available at `https://github.com/ethereum/web3.py`.
- If you are an avid Java user, the Java library is available on the Web3J GitHub account, which can be found at `https://github.com/web3j/web3j`.

For any other implementations, you can find the libraries under the Ethereum GitHub account at `https://github.com/ethereum/`. Golem is a great example of using Ethereum outside your browser. We have already taken a look at this in the first chapter. Golem computes off-chain, but verifies all the computing that has been done on-chain. This allows a massive amount of distributed computing power. For further information, you can refer to the Golem Github page and check out the codes in the repository at `https://github.com/golemfactory/golem`.

Ethereum and IoT

In this section, we are going to take a look at Ethereum and how it helps propagate the IoT. In my personal opinion, Ethereum is the perfect backbone for IoT. This is because of two factors: dataflow and security. Data is spread out across the network, which is the most basic concept of IoT; this unhindered and smooth flow of data is an essential factor in using Ethereum to help build the IoT. Also, every device has its own private key that enhances the security factor. The combination of these two elements opens up a lot of new possibilities.

Let us look at a case study involving the charging of electric vehicles. At this moment, they are not many electric vehicles or charging stations. There is a high possibility that all vehicles will run on electricity in the near future. This would mean that more charging stations will be placed at many more locations. Let us consider a scenario where there are charging stations at a supermarket. It wouldn't be feasible to provide this facility for free. To make this process easier, the car could pay for the service directly. How does one do this?

There have to be two smart meters, each with their own private keys. One is on the charging station while the other one is on the car. The owner/user of the car needs to add some ethers to the address that is associated with the private key of the car. When the car requests electricity at a charging station, this would be added to the smart contract that is in charge of this transaction. The smart meter at the charging station would track the charge that has been consumed by the car and charge it accordingly. The amount here would be paid directly. The owner of the charging station would then withdraw the ethers as required.

This whole scenario, though hypothetical for now, has some special considerations. Both the car and charging station will need a computer because they each need to have a private key. There also needs to be a working internet connection and some tamper proof smart meters. Once the data is on the blockchain, no one can tamper with it, as it is all a part of public records. Even if the tamper proof meters have a flaw, it will be displayed publicly. Another way to avoid fraud would be to register the car's private key with the relevant authorities.

Ethereum and smartphone applications

You can make smartphone applications with Ethereum support in three ways:

- Using a DApp browser.
- Using Android or the iOS library.
- Doing everything in JavaScript, from key generation to key security and everything in-between. However, this is not recommended, as this makes you very vulnerable.

Using a DApp browser

One kind of DApp browser is Toshi. It will allow you to make use of the centralized application, and you can use it in pretty much the same way in which you would use MetaMask, but on a mobile. Another more popular option is Status.IM. It's actually a secure chat, but it's also a chat bot. You can give it commands such as retrieving the browser location, as shown in the following screenshot, and if you give it such commands, then you can trigger functions inside of the smart contracts:

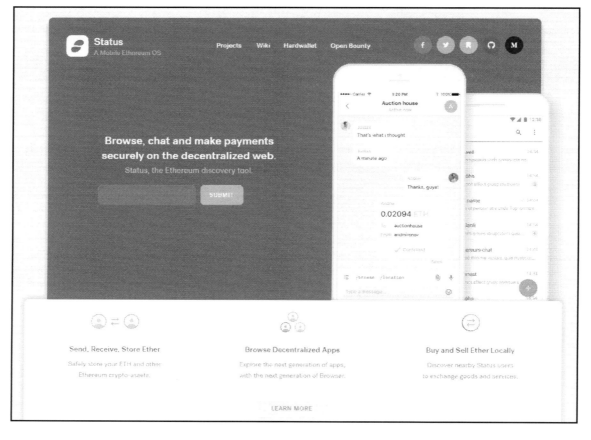

Status.IM home page

A few applications have been developed using this method. One such application is **WhoPays**. This a contract-based bot that creates groups in which users can keep track of their payments to a group through commands using a new chat bot. What this means is that you can use chat commands to set up the group. Suppose you bought groceries for three people and you paid for everything. Others have to pay you back. You can set this arrangement up, and they can agree to an amount and pay you back using the application. The following screenshot shows the **WhoPays** GitHub page at `https://github.com/Nielsvdiermen/WhoPays`:

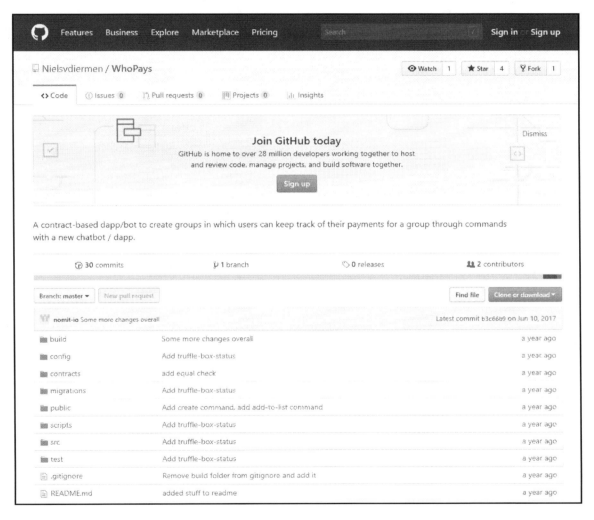

WhoPays

Another example is `favor.network`. Here, you can request favors from people and pay them to fulfill those favors:

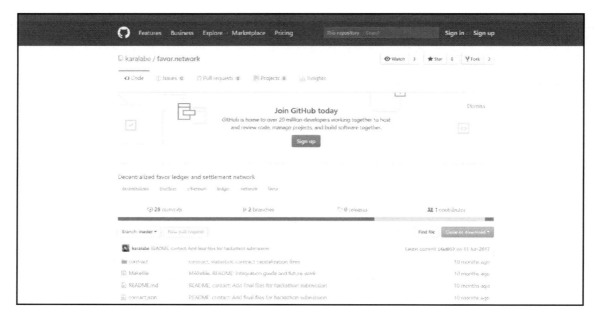

Favor.network

These applications either won or were placed very high at the `Status.IM` Hackathon. I highly recommend that you check these applications out and use them to learn exactly how you can work with `Status.IM`.

Using Android or the iOS library

In December 2016, Ethereum released a version of their desktop client that also works on mobile platforms so that you can just import these libraries into your Android application or your iOS application and use Ethereum in the same way that you would use it on a desktop.

The following screenshot shows the go-ethereum GitHub repository at `https://github.com/ethereum/go-ethereum/wiki/Building-Ethereum`:

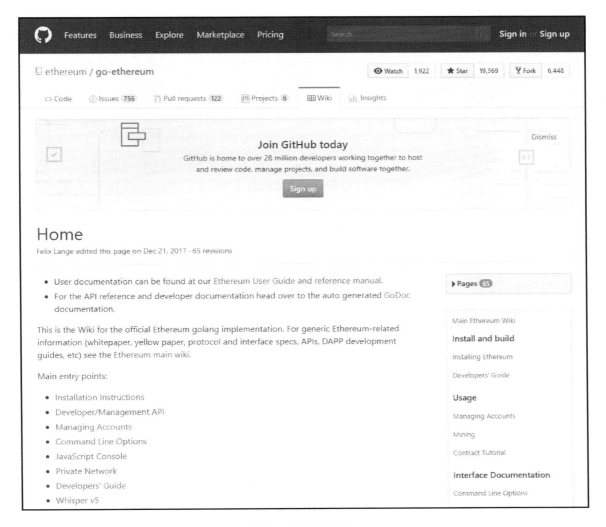

Go-Ethereum GitHub repository

Further steps and resources

I want to mention Infura. Infura is basically a relay server for the Ethereum and IPFS network that you don't have to manage yourself, making it trustless again. This will exist pretty much for as long as some people are not running their own Ethereum node. Visit www.infura.io for more information. It is of course highly recommended that you run your own nodes, but in case you can't, check out Infura. You can remotely send resigned transactions to this server and they will propagate them into the network.

Another resource for you to check out is the Ethereum GitHub page, which we have mentioned before. Here, you can find all the projects, such as the Ethereum Improvement Protocol, the remix, and yellow paper, which has all the technical specifications of Ethereum. You can find out everything about the Solidity programming language and the different clients that have been built. You can adapt these clients and then use them in your own projects to connect to the Ethereum network. So just check it out!

Another source of information is the Ethereum Subreddit, which you can find at www.reddit.com/r/ethereum/. You can find a lot of info and a lot of news here; something for you to check out if you want to keep up to date.

Another resource is CoinDesk you can find at www.coindesk.com. You probably know this one, but this has a lot of news regarding not only Ethereum, but everything blockchain.

Consensys is a company, which you can find at https://new.consensys.net/. They have been leveraging Ethereum pretty much since its inception, and they have a lot of projects that they are working on. They partner with a lot of very big companies, such as Microsoft. They are pretty much committed to making Ethereum enterprise-ready.

Last but not least, do check out State Of The DApps, which you can find at www.stateofthedapps.com. Here, you can find a lot of applications that have been made. You can sort through them and see if they have any prototypes, or maybe some live applications. Almost all of these applications are open source. This is going to be by far your biggest resource because what better way is there to learn than from existing applications, right? So, if you check these out, I'm sure you will be well on your way to totally mastering Ethereum very soon.

Summary

In this chapter, we understood how Ethereum is run outside the browser. We learnt how Ethereum can be used for various IoT applications. Then we went on to see how Ethereum is implemented on smartphone devices in Android as well as iOS using various methods. Then you were given some links to various resources that can help you master Ethereum. In this book, we have covered almost everything that you need to build, use, and deploy your own Ethereum token, and have given you additional insight into what applications you can build with this knowledge of Ethereum.

Other Books You May Enjoy

If you enjoyed this book, you may be interested in these other books by Packt:

Hands-On Blockchain with Hyperledger
Nitin Gaur et al.

ISBN: 978-1-78899-452-1

- Discover why blockchain is a game changer in the technology landscape
- Set up blockchain networks using basic Hyperledger Fabric deployment
- Understand the considerations for creating decentralized applications
- Learn to integrate business networks with existing systems
- Write Smart Contracts quickly with Hyperledger Composer
- Design transaction model and chaincode with Golang

Mastering Blockchain - Second Edition
Imran Bashir

ISBN: 978-1-78883-904-4

- Master the theoretical and technical foundations of the blockchain technology
- Understand the concept of decentralization, its impact, and its relationship with blockchain technology
- Master how cryptography is used to secure data - with practical examples
- Grasp the inner workings of blockchain and the mechanisms behind bitcoin and alternative cryptocurrencies
- Understand the theoretical foundations of smart contracts
- Learn how Ethereum blockchain works and how to develop decentralized applications using Solidity and relevant development frameworks

Leave a review - let other readers know what you think

Please share your thoughts on this book with others by leaving a review on the site that you bought it from. If you purchased the book from Amazon, please leave us an honest review on this book's Amazon page. This is vital so that other potential readers can see and use your unbiased opinion to make purchasing decisions, we can understand what our customers think about our products, and our authors can see your feedback on the title that they have worked with Packt to create. It will only take a few minutes of your time, but is valuable to other potential customers, our authors, and Packt. Thank you!

Index

Made in the USA
Columbia, SC
25 October 2018